The Magic of MERLIN

HE·WHO·PULLS
THE·SWORD·FROM·
THIS·STONE·IS
RIGHTFUL
KING·
OF
ENGLAND·

by Stephanie Spinner
illustrated by Valerie Sokolova

For Rena
S.S.

To my loving husband, Sasha
V.S.

Library of Congress Cataloging-in-Publication Data
Spinner, Stephanie.
The magic of Merlin / by Stephanie Spinner ; illustrated by Valerie Sokolova.
     p.   cm. — (Road to reading. Mile 4)
Summary: Merlin the wizard helps England's King Uther win the
lady he loves and in exchange the king gives Merlin his son to
protect and raise to be a great future king.
ISBN 0-307-46403-2 (GB). — ISBN 0-307-26403-3 (pbk.)
1. Merlin (Legendary character) Juvenile fiction. 2. Arthur, King Juvenile fiction.
[1. Merlin (Legendary character) Fiction. 2. Arthur, King Fiction.
3. Magic Fiction.]
I. Sokolova, Valerie, ill. II. Title. III. Series.
PZ7. S7567Mag 2000   99-34415
[Fic]—dc21   CIP

A GOLDEN BOOK · New York
Golden Books Publishing Company, Inc.
New York, New York 10106

ISBN: 0-307-26403-3 (pbk)   A MM
ISBN: 0-307-46403-2 (GB)

CONTENTS

Merlin the Wizard

Long, long ago, in ancient England, magic was as real as the ocean and as strong as the tides. Many longed to use it. Few had the gift.

One who did was Merlin.

As a child, Merlin was quiet. He thought and watched more than he spoke. But when he spoke, people learned to listen. He could look into the past. He could see into the future. He could work powerful magic.

By the time he was grown, even the king knew his name.

Chapter One

King Uther ruled all England. He
was a brave knight and a good king. He
led the country well. Yet he could not
win the heart of the woman he loved.

One day he called for Merlin.

"I wish to marry the Lady Igraine,"
he said. "But she will not have me. Is it
within your power to change her mind?"

"It is," said Merlin. "Within a month she will be your queen. And in time she will bear you a son."

These words pleased the king. "If this comes to pass," he told Merlin, "I will give you whatever you wish."

"When it comes to pass, I will remember your promise," said Merlin.

Merlin worked his magic. Within a month the Lady Igraine became King Uther's wife. Soon they had a son. His name was Arthur.

At this time Merlin appeared before the king. "My lord," he said, "do you remember your promise to me?"

"I do," said the king. "What is it you wish?"

Merlin's answer was a single word. "Arthur," he said.

King Uther grew pale. "My son?" he asked.

"Yes," said Merlin. "One day your son will be a great king. But not before much blood is shed. I have seen the future. Your death comes soon. And with it come dark times. I will keep the boy safe."

King Uther saw the wisdom of Merlin's request. He nodded. Merlin took Arthur and disappeared.

Chapter Two

A year later King Uther died. His throne sat empty, and peace left England. A dark time began.

Merlin found a home for Arthur with a knight called Sir Ector. Arthur grew into a strong young boy. He knew nothing of his real parents, or of Merlin.

6

But Merlin knew Arthur. He watched the boy in secret and liked what he saw. Arthur was kind. He was brave. He fought fairly.

One day, when Arthur was seventeen years old, Merlin saw the future. Arthur was wearing a crown and holding a sword.

The boy's time has come, thought Merlin. He went to a church near London. That night—the longest of the year—he cast a powerful spell.

A great stone appeared in the churchyard. Rising out of the stone was a sword.

These words were carved on the stone:

"He who pulls the sword from this stone is rightful king of England."

News of the magical sword spread quickly. Merlin let it be known that a tournament would be held on New Year's Day. All who fought in it could try their hand at the sword.

Soon knights from all over England came riding into London. Among them were Sir Ector and his two sons, Kay and Arthur. Kay had just become a knight. Now he was Sir Kay—and eager to prove his strength.

On the day of the tournament, Kay hurried to the fighting field. In his haste he left his sword behind at the inn.

"Fetch it for me," he told Arthur. "And quickly! The tournament starts soon."

Arthur rode to the inn. He found it locked, for everyone had gone to the tournament. Arthur was troubled. How would Kay fight without a sword?

He passed the churchyard, and a glint of silver caught his eye. It was the sword in the stone. "Here is a fine weapon for Kay!" said Arthur. He quickly drew the sword from the stone and carried it back to the tournament.

Chapter Three

Arthur gave the sword to his brother.
"It is not your sword," he said. "Still,
it is a fine weapon. I found it in the
churchyard."

Kay stared at the sword. "The
churchyard?" he said. He showed the
sword to Sir Ector.

"Arthur!" cried Sir Ector. "How did

13

you get this sword?"

"I drew it from a stone—so Kay could enter the tournament."

"Will you show me how you did it?" asked Sir Ector. There was a look on his face Arthur had never seen before. Surprise, sorrow, and joy—all mixed together.

"Yes," said Arthur.

In the churchyard, Arthur replaced the sword. Sir Ector tried to pull it from the stone. He could not.

Then Sir Kay took hold of the sword. He pulled and pulled. The sword felt like part of the rock. It would not move.

"Now you, Arthur," said Sir Ector.

"It is easily done," said Arthur. And
so it was. As Ector and Kay watched,
Arthur drew the sword from the stone.

"Here," he said, holding it out to them. They fell to their knees.

"Father!" cried Arthur. "Kay! What are you doing?"

"I raised you, but you are not my son," said Sir Ector. "You were given to me by Merlin. And now I know why. You are meant to be king."

"Merlin?" asked Arthur. "Who is he?"

A man in dark robes appeared from behind the stone, as if he had been waiting. "I am Merlin," he said. "And the words on the stone are for you."

"I—I cannot read them," said Arthur.

"Look again," said Merlin.

He raised his hand. The letters on the stone moved and swirled. Then they became still—and suddenly their meaning was clear.

HE·WHO·PULLS·
THE·SWORD·FROM·
THIS·STONE·IS
RIGHTFUL·
KING
OF
ENGLAND

"King of England!" gasped Arthur. *How can I be king?* he thought. *I am young. I have grown up on a farm. I know nothing of ruling!*

Arthur looked at Merlin. He saw a man who always spoke the truth.

"When I am king," said Arthur, "will you counsel me and be my friend?"

"I will," said Merlin.

Arthur's fears fell away. "Then all will be well," he said.

Chapter Four

Arthur became king. Peace was
slow in coming back to England. The
country was full of lawless men. There
were many who did not wish to be
ruled by someone so young. There
were others who plotted to take back
the throne.

Merlin helped Arthur in many ways.

Sometimes he helped with advice. Sometimes he helped with magic. He saved Arthur's life more than once.

One day Arthur was riding through the forest by himself. Merlin had warned him against this. "You are king," he said, "not some simple knight!

You put yourself in danger when you ride alone." There were times when Arthur did not heed Merlin. This was one of them.

As he went on his way, Arthur heard angry shouts. Then Merlin appeared, running from three men with knives and clubs.

"Give us your money, old man!" cried one of the men.

"Or we'll beat it out of you!" swore another.

Merlin stumbled and fell. The men were about to attack him when Arthur rode up. "Flee, churls!" he shouted.

The men saw a knight in armor on a big horse. The horse reared. The knight raised his sword. The men ran in fright.

"Well, Merlin," said Arthur, raising his helmet, "it seems I have saved you when magic could not." He smiled. "Have you lost your powers?"

Merlin had one secret. He could use his magic to protect others. But he could not use it on himself. He did not want anyone to know this, for it would put him in great danger. So he said, "You are closer to death than I," and walked on in silence.

Before Arthur could ask what Merlin meant, they came to a clearing in the forest. The shields of many knights hung from the trees. The grass was red with blood. "It seems many have done battle here," said Arthur.

Just then a knight rode into the clearing. He was the tallest man Arthur

had ever seen. "Turn back or fight!"
the knight said.

"Who challenges me?" asked Arthur.

"I am Sir Pellinore," said the knight.
"And I will soon take your shield. No
man has won against me yet."

"I would like to be the first," said Arthur. Sir Pellinore simply laughed. Then he and Arthur charged at each other with such force that their lances broke. They jumped off their horses. Drawing their swords from their scabbards, they struck at each other again and again.

Now the clearing rang with the clash of metal—a sound so harsh it drove the birds from the trees. Soon Arthur and Pellinore were covered in blood. They stopped to rest, then fought again.

With a mighty blow, Sir Pellinore broke Arthur's sword in two.

"Surrender," he said, forcing Arthur to the ground.

"I will not," said Arthur.

Sir Pellinore did not know he was fighting the king. "Then you must die," he said. He pulled off Arthur's helmet and raised his sword. Arthur remembered Merlin's words. *I am indeed close to death,* he thought.

Merlin stepped forward quickly. He cast a spell on Sir Pellinore. The knight fell into a sudden sleep. His huge body toppled to the ground. It lay there like a fallen tree.

Arthur sat up slowly, for he was in pain. "I hope you have not slain him, Merlin," he gasped. "He is a fighter of great skill."

"I only cast a spell on him," said Merlin. "He will wake from it unharmed. But your wounds are deep," he said, helping Arthur to stand. "They will take three days to heal."

"Three days!" groaned Arthur.

"Alas! That is the best my magic can do," said Merlin. And now it was his turn to smile.

Chapter Five

Arthur's wounds healed in three days. When he was strong again, he spoke to Merlin. "Now I have no sword," he said, "for Sir Pellinore broke mine in two. I must get another. It is not fitting for a king to go unarmed." Arthur wished to fight Sir Pellinore again, but he kept that to himself.

"You shall have a sword this very day," said Merlin. He led Arthur to a lake that gleamed blue, then silver, then green. Out of the bright water rose an arm. In its hand was a sword, shining like a piece of the moon. The sight made Arthur's breath stop.

Near the sword a young woman appeared. Her robes glistened blue, then silver, then green. "Who is she?" asked Arthur in a whisper.

"She is the Lady of the Lake," said Merlin. "The sword belongs to her."

The lady's hair was golden. Her face was young and fair. "Good day, King Arthur," she said.

"Good day, my lady," said Arthur. "Your sword is most wonderful. I—I wish it were mine, for I have none."

"The sword shall be yours," said the lady, "if you promise to return it before you die."

"I promise," said Arthur.

"Then row onto the lake," she said. "Take the sword and its scabbard. They will serve you well." The water rippled and she was gone.

Chapter Six

A wooden barge waited at the shore.
Arthur and Merlin rowed to the center
of the lake. When they were close
enough, Arthur reached for the sword.
It came into his hand quickly, as if it
were alive.

Merlin rowed back to the shore.
Arthur turned the sword this way and

that. Its hilt sparkled with jewels. Its blade flashed like lightning. "This is a wondrous weapon. I long to try it," said Arthur, thinking of Sir Pellinore.

Merlin knew exactly what Arthur was thinking. "Do you see this scabbard?" he asked.

"Yes," said Arthur, though his eyes were on the sword.

"It does not flash or shine," said Merlin, "but the scabbard is worth ten swords. If you wear it when you fight, you will lose no blood—no matter how deep your wounds. Keep it with you always."

They mounted their horses. Instead of turning toward home, Arthur rode back into the forest. "I would fight Sir Pellinore again," he told Merlin. "This time cast no spells, I pray you."

"This time there is no need," said Merlin.

Arthur and Sir Pellinore fought once more, first with their lances, then with their swords. Sir Pellinore struck Arthur with such force that the ground shook. Arthur did not bleed, for he wore the scabbard.

Then Arthur's new sword cut through Sir Pellinore's armor. The big knight fell, bleeding. He tried to get up. He could not.

"Will you spare my life?" he asked Arthur.

Arthur drew off his helmet. "If you pledge to serve me from this day forth," he said.

"You have my pledge," said Sir Pellinore. "Tell me your name."

"He is Arthur, your king," said Merlin.

Sir Pellinore pulled himself to his feet. He bowed to Arthur. "Your majesty! I thank you for your mercy," he said.

"I hope that every knight who joins me is as bold and strong as you," said Arthur. Suddenly Merlin saw the future once again. Arthur sat at a round table with the bravest knights in England. Their eyes were on him. Their hearts were with him.

The dark times are over, thought Merlin. And he was glad.

Merlin the Fool

The years passed. Arthur became a great king, and Merlin's magic helped him time after time.

Then a beautiful young woman learned Merlin's secrets. She cast a spell on him and hid him from the world. Merlin could do nothing to stop her. Now he lies deep underground, halfway between death and dreaming.

All those who read Merlin's story, heed this advice: Be wary of magic!

Author's Note

Did Arthur and Merlin really exist?
There are many wonderful old
stories, songs, and poems about King
Arthur and his knights. A book from
1136, *A History of the Kings of Britain*,
describes Arthur as a British warrior
king of the fifth century. But that book
was written almost seven hundred
years after his time.

And Merlin remains a mystery.